# Words of Freemasonry:

## A Weekly Guide to Self-Improvement

**WB Robert S. Dilworth**

To request permission, contact the publisher keystoneppllc@gmail.com

Paperback: ISBN 979-8-9896828-0-5
eBook: ISBN 979-8-9896828-3-6
Library of Congress Number 2023952595
First paperback edition August 2024
Editor: Seth Hunter
Book Cover By: Umar All
Proofreader: Adegoke Omolara
Layout Design Editor: Maryam Sadiqa
Company Logo Designer: Aquil Akhter
Publishers Webpage: https://keystoneppllc.com

# Disclaimer

This book is for information purposes only. It does not purport to represent the Grand Lodge of the Most Ancient and Honorable Society of Free and Accepted Masons of the State of New Jersey or any other Grand Lodge. The information contained in this book does not reflect the views or opinions of any lodge affiliation or jurisdiction. Additionally, any persons, lodges, or situations depicted in this book are fictional and used solely for information.

**To**

_____

_____

**From**

_____

_____

**On**

_____

_____

# Table of Contents

About The Author ................................................ I

Acknowledgment................................................III

Introduction ..................................................... V

Chapter 1 .........................................................1

A Weekly Guide..................................................1

Chapter 2 .........................................................4

Seven Steps To Self-Improvement ......................4

Chapter 3 .........................................................8

Self-Affirmation.................................................8

Chapter 4 .......................................................10

Freemasonry ...................................................10

Chapter 5 .......................................................13

Masonic Words ................................................13

Chapter 6 .......................................................29

Morality ..........................................................29

Chapter 7 .......................................................33

Allegory ..........................................................33

Chapter 8 .......................................................36

Esoteric Vs. Exoteric.......................................36

Chapter 9 .......................................................39

Square ...................................................... 39

Chapter 10 ............................................... 41

Compasses ............................................... 41

Chapter 11 ............................................... 44

Entered Apprentice .................................... 44

Chapter 12 ............................................... 47

Fellow Craft ............................................. 47

Chapter 13 ............................................... 49

Master Mason ........................................... 49

Chapter 14 ............................................... 52

The Volume Of Scared Law ........................ 52

Chapter 15 ............................................... 54

Level ....................................................... 54

Chapter 16 ............................................... 56

Plumb ..................................................... 56

Chapter 17 ............................................... 58

Wisdom, Strength, And Beauty .................. 58

Chapter 18 ............................................... 60

Fortitude Prudence Temperance And Justice ..... 60

Chapter 19 ............................................... 63

Brotherly Love, Relief, And Truth .............. 63

Chapter 20 ............................................... 65

Obligation ............................................... 65

Chapter 21 ................................................ 67

Prayer ..................................................... 67

Chapter 22 ................................................ 69

The Letter "G" ........................................... 69

Chapter 23 ................................................ 72

47th Problem Of Euclid ................................ 72

Chapter 24 ................................................ 74

The All-Seeing Eye .................................... 74

Chapter 25 ................................................ 76

Operative Masonry ..................................... 76

Chapter 26 ................................................ 79

Speculative Masonry ................................... 79

Chapter 27 ................................................ 82

Rough And Perfect Ashlar ........................... 82

Chapter 28 ................................................ 85

Chamber Of Reflection ............................... 85

Chapter 29 ................................................ 88

King Solomon's Temple .............................. 88

Chapter 30 ................................................ 91

Blue Lodge .............................................. 91

Chapter 31 ................................................ 93

Clandestine Masonry .................................. 93

Chapter 32 ................................................ 96

The Craft............................................................ 96

Chapter 33 ......................................................... 98

Faith, Hope, And Charity ................................ 98

Chapter 34 ........................................................ 101

Seven Liberal Arts And Sciences .................... 101

Chapter 35 ........................................................ 103

Masonic Ritual ................................................. 103

Chapter 36 ........................................................ 105

Point Within The Circle .................................. 105

Chapter 37 ........................................................ 108

Three Distinct Knocks ..................................... 108

Chapter 38 ........................................................ 110

Of My Own Free Will And Accord ................. 110

Chapter 39 ........................................................ 112

Masonic Education ........................................... 112

Chapter 40 ........................................................ 114

Masonic Leadership ......................................... 114

Chapter 41 ........................................................ 119

Fraternity ......................................................... 119

Chapter 42 ........................................................ 122

Prince Hall ....................................................... 122

Chapter 43 ........................................................ 125

Ancient Landmarks ......................................... 125

Chapter 44............................................ 127

Making Good Men Better .............................. 127

Chapter 45............................................ 130

Worshipful Master.................................... 130

Chapter 46............................................ 132

Senior Warden ....................................... 132

Chapter 47............................................ 134

Junior Warden ....................................... 134

Chapter 48............................................ 136

Lambskin Apron...................................... 136

Chapter 49............................................ 138

Signs And Symbols ................................... 138

Chapter 50............................................ 141

Broken Column ...................................... 141

Chapter 51............................................ 143

Past Master .......................................... 143

Chapter 52............................................ 145

Most Worshipful Grand Master ....................... 145

References ........................................... 148

# About The Author

Right Worshipful Past Grand Chaplain Grand Lodge of The State of New Jersey.

Past Master Historic Alpha Lodge No 116 F&AM.

North Jersey Past Masters Masonic Association.

Society of King Solomon, Distinguished Fellow Grand Lodge of the State of New Jersey.

Past High Priest Alpha Chapter No.62 RAM.

Past Grand Chaplain, Grand Royal Arch Chapter of the State of New Jersey.

Past District Deputy Grand High Priest, Grand Royal Arch Chapter of the State of New Jersey.

Junius C. H. Schmidt Distinguish Service Award, Grand Royal Arch Chapter of The State of New Jersey.

Charter Member St. Andrew Council No.18 Royal and Select Masters.

Jerusalem Commandery No. 32

Northern NJ Council No.10 Knight Masons, U.S.A

Past Thrice Potent Master Lodge of Perfection-Valley of Northern NJ AASR.

Executive Council Member Valley of Northern New Jersey

Ancient Accepted Scottish Rite 32° Northern Masonic Jurisdiction USA.

Hauts Grades Academy Graduate AASR, NMJ USA

Past Sovereign Master Alexandria Council No. 478 Allied Masonic Degrees.

St Joseph Conclave Knights of the Red Cross of Constantine.

Haggi Chapter Mark Master Masons.

The New Jersey Lodge of Masonic Research and Education Number 1786.

Shriners International.

# Acknowledgment

I want to express my deepest gratitude to all those who have supported me during the creation of this book. I want to thank my mother, a single parent raising three outstanding men, who taught us the importance of education and not only to work hard but also to be smart... Love you, mom. To my daughter, Anivia, for encouraging me to author this book and wanting to be the first to read the transcript. My sons Robert III and Nuri, thank you for making me proud to be your father, and to my grandchildren, I am praying for a better and safer world for you. I want to thank my two brothers, Dave, and Arthur, for always being there for me in the good and tough times. I am forever indebted to my brother from another mother, Mark Ali Shabazz El, for signing my petition and introducing me to Freemasonry. The humblest gratitude bestowed upon Most Worshipful John Eugene Margroff, Grand Master of Masons for the State of New Jersey, for appointing me, Grand Chaplain.

I would also like to thank my Editor Seth Hunter for his invaluable feedback and guidance, and for taking the time to read early drafts of the manuscript and provide insightful comments. Also I would like to give all the praise to my Layout Design Editor Maryam Sadiqa without her this book would never been published and my proofreader Adegoke Omolara, my book cover designer Umar Ali fantastic creation. I am grateful for the support and encouragement from my colleagues and friends, especially the brethren of Historic Alpha Lodge No. 116 F&AM. Alpha Strong!

Finally, I would like to acknowledge the financial support from Keystone Publishing and Promotions LLC, which made this book's creation possible. I appreciate Aquil Akhter, the logo designer for Keystone Publishing and Promotion LLC.

I hope readers will receive this book well and contribute meaningfully to Freemasonry. Thank you for participating in this journey through Words of Freemasonry and Self Improvement.

# Introduction

When we joined Freemasonry, most of us did it as an opportunity to improve ourselves. You heard the claim made by most Grand Lodges, "We make good men better," which is quite attractive, but one thing they insist on ignoring is the word "Self-Improvement."

Freemasonry contains lessons from generation to generation, improving men worldwide. Therefore, self-esteem begins from within, starting with a genuine desire for self-improvement. At its heart, Freemasonry is a profoundly personal pursuit and means something different to its initiates. It is a commitment by an individual to value the time-honored system of personal development of the mind, body, and soul.

**Words of Freemasonry: A Weekly Guide to Self-Improvement** is for anyone seeking personal development. Words are beautiful, ugly, and sometimes quite deceptive, depending on their literal meanings and how they sound, look, and are used. The book's primary purpose is to apply the teaching of freemasonry to one's daily life. It is to be used as a guide, reference, or journal.

I have created Words of Freemasonry: A Weekly Guide to Self-Improvement to foster a better understanding of Masonic words, terms, phrases, and philosophy through group sessions, lodges, lectures, workshops, seminars, book clubs, and one-on-one discussions. Words of Freemasonry: A Weekly Guide to Self-Improvement is a perfect gift for the newly raised Mason. It is a great introduction to those wanting to learn more about this ancient craft known as Freemasonry. Every chapter entails real-life situations displaying Freemasonry as a practice to use daily. It will assist lodges in developing an educational program and much more.

Freemasonry is a fraternity that emphasizes the values of brotherhood, charity, and self-improvement. Masonic education is a vital aspect of the organization and aims to help members develop and improve themselves in numerous ways.

One of the primary ways Masonry promotes self-improvement is through moral and ethical teachings. Masons are encouraged to live moral lives, such as honesty, integrity, and fairness, which are essential to personal growth and self-improvement. They also study and reflect on the symbolic lessons of the craft, which provides a deeper understanding of themselves and the world around them.

Another way Masonry promotes self-improvement is through its emphasis on education and learning. Masons are encouraged to continue their education and seek new knowledge. They have access to various educational resources, including books, lectures, and classes, which can help develop new skills, broaden their perspectives, and improve their understanding of the world. In addition, Masons are encouraged to take an active role in their communities and use their skills and knowledge to help others. It allows individuals to feel a sense of purpose and fulfillment and encourages a sense of civic responsibility.

So, I encourage you to join me in this journey of Words of Freemasonry: A Weekly Guide to Self–Improvement.

**"Words are powerful. They can create, or they can destroy. So, choose your words wisely."**

WB Robert S. Dilworth
Author

# Chapter 1
# A Weekly Guide

**Words of Freemasonry**: **A Weekly Guide to Self-Improvement** has words associated with Freemasonry. Words can be beautiful, ugly, and sometimes quite deceptive, depending on their literal meanings and how they sound, look, and are used.

Chapter 2 will teach you the **Seven Steps to Self-Improvement**. Chapter 3 introduces the reader to **Self-Affirmations**, which are highly recommended for Self-Improvement.

The assignments begin in chapter 4 "Freemasonry,". Every chapter starts with a Masonic word (e.g., Freemasonry), which is defined and described in real-life situations. Strengths and weaknesses are explored. Lastly, how can the teachings of Masonry be applied? Here are some examples of a real-life situation using the application of Freemasonry:

**Week 1**: Brotherly Love in Freemasonry, the bond of brotherly love is considered the foundation of all moral virtues. This week, I will focus on developing my relationships with others by being kind, understanding, and forgiving. To practice empathy and try to see things from the perspective of others.

**Week 2**: Relief, in the context of Freemasonry, refers to helping those in need. This week, I focus on ways to give back to my community through donating, volunteering, or simply being there for someone in need. Remember, the most significant measure of a man's success is not what he has but what he gives.

**Week 3**: Truth in Freemasonry, truth is considered a central tenet. This week, strive to be honest with yourself and others. Practice self-reflection and seek to understand your motivations and actions. Please try to be truthful, even when it is complicated.

**Week 4**: Wisdom is the ability based on a deep understanding of life. This week, I will seek out new experiences and opportunities for learning. Read books, attend lectures, or converse with people with different perspectives and ideas. Pursuing wisdom is a lifelong journey, and every new experience brings you closer to understanding the world around you.

A Weekly Guide provides a framework for self-improvement, and it is essential to remember that self-improvement requires dedication and effort. The principles of Freemasonry can be a valuable source of inspiration and guidance, but one must always strive to become a better person.

Once the book is completed, you will accomplish the following:

1. Establish a journal.
2. Enhance vocabulary and a better understanding of Masonic words and their meaning.

3. Knowledge of the seven Steps of Self-Improvement.
4. How Self Affirmations contribute to personal growth.
5. Recognizing self-improvement as a core value in Freemasonry.

As a critical reminder, everyone receives an A+. No one fails. So, let us say a particular chapter was challenging; remember, if you tried, you succeeded! In life, we learn many things from our failures. The only actual loss is giving up. If you did not finish an assignment or do not have time to finish the book, it is all right. When you do, start where you left off or complete the Weekly Guide after each chapter. The weekly lessons are fun but challenging, aiming at measurable outcomes denoting strengths and weaknesses. Remember, in life, we only get out what we put in.

# Chapter 2
# 7 Steps to Self-Improvement

The new Oxford American Dictionary (Oxford University Press, 2010) defines self-improvement as improving oneself through conscious efforts, typically by developing one's abilities, qualities, or performance in a particular area. In other words, self-improvement is the ongoing development and growth of one's skills, knowledge, personal qualities, and general well-being. It includes learning new skills, setting and achieving personal objectives, engaging in self-reflection, and taking care of one's physical and mental health. The goal of self-improvement is to become the best version of oneself, leading to a more fulfilling and satisfying life.

## 7   Steps to Self-Improvement

1. **Set realistic daily goals that are meaningful to you**.

   You will never change your life until you change something you do daily. Identify areas for improvement: Take a self-assessment and identify areas of your life that you want to improve. This could be related to your relationships, career, health, personal growth, etc.

> *"The secret to your success is in your daily routine."* John C. Maxwell

2. **Create an action plan you can follow**.

   Create a plan of action that outlines how you will achieve each step. Set specific, measurable objectives: Define what you want to achieve and set clear goals to help you reach your desired outcome. Make sure these plans are realistic and achievable.

> *"We are what we repeatedly do. Excellence, then, is not an act but a habit."* Aristotle

3. **Take one day at a time**.

   Be patient and persistent: Self-improvement takes time and effort, and it is essential to be patient and persistent in your efforts. Celebrate your successes and use setbacks as opportunities to gain experience and grow.

   When asked what surprised him most about humanity, the Dalai Lama answered, *"Man sacrifices his health to make money, then he sacrifices money to recuperate his health. And then he is so anxious about the future that he does not enjoy the present, the result being that he does not live in the present or future; he lives as if he is never going to die and then dies having never really lived."*

4. **Keep track of your successes**.

Focus on your successes: Focus on developing and leveraging your strengths rather than solely trying to fix your weaknesses. This will help you achieve your goals more efficiently and effectively.

*"Success is peace of mind directly resulting from self-satisfaction in knowing you did your best to become the best you can be."*
John Wooden

5. **Stay optimistic.**

Always keep a positive mindset and surround yourself with supportive people who will encourage and motivate you on your journey toward self-improvement.

*"Yesterday is history, and tomorrow is a mystery; today is a gift of God, which is why we call it the present."* Bill Keane

6. **Practice Self Affirmation (Self-Talk).**

Embrace personal growth: Be open to learning, trying new experiences, and accepting feedback. Personal growth often comes from stepping outside of your comfort zone.
**I AM That I AM**... What you put after **I AM**, you become.

7. **Always be mindful and aware of self-doubt and procrastination.**

    Choose to focus your time, energy, and activities around people who uplift you, love you, and encourage improvement, which develops the happiest, most robust, wisest version of your "Self."

    *"The greatest barrier to success is the fear of failure."*- Sven Goran Eriksson.

# Chapter 3
# Self-Affirmation

Self-affirmation (self-talk) is affirming one's worthiness and value as an individual for beneficial effects such as increasing one's confidence or self-esteem. Self-affirmation helps you concentrate on achieving your goals and allows you to remove negative thoughts and replace them with positive ones, eventually leading to a new belief system. Self-affirmation leads to a productive life.

**"I AM"** are two of the most powerful words today. What you put after them, you become. Using the two words **"I AM"** in self-affirmation means you are making a powerful declaration. You can use affirmations to develop your subconscious mind to bring about those statements you declare in your life. **"I AM"** self-affirmation helps us to affirm who we are, who we want to be, and how we want to feel. Imagine an image of self-affirmations to help with your purpose and then post them around the house, office, phones, journals, or anything visible.

In John's gospel, Jesus made seven profound **"I AM"** statements (**I AM** the bread of life.... the light of the world ...the door...the Good Shepherd...the resurrection and the life... the way, the truth, and the life.... the true vine..."). Jesus identified himself as the great **"I AM."**

God revealed his name to Moses in the Old Testament as **"I AM WHO I AM."** You are to say this to the Israelites; **"I AM** has sent me to you (Exodus 3:14). Thus, in Judaism,**" I AM"** is unquestionably understood as a name for God.

Verses from the Holy Quran, "Indeed, **I AM** Allah, there is no deity (No God) except Me, so worship Me and establish prayer for My remembrance. (20:14).

Seven Self-affirmations are quoted daily for self-improvement.

- **I AM THAT I AM.**
- **I AM** going to believe in myself.
- **I AM** (Recite the goal)
- **I AM** willing to learn from my mistakes.
- **I AM** able to accomplish anything I set my mind to.
- **I AM** learning to respect the process when I do not understand it.
- **I AM** seeking spirituality.

# Chapter 4
# Freemasonry

Freemasonry is a beautiful/peculiar system of morality veiled in allegory and illustrated with/by symbols. Freemasonry, in its simplest form, is a philosophy or teaching that enables a person to improve and equip himself for life's tempestuous sea of troubles. Freemasonry's core value is self-improvement.

Freemasonry elicits words that remind a Mason to strive toward perfection. The result is becoming a better man today than he was yesterday. When applying Freemasonry, Masons learned the importance of spiritually becoming a better husband, father, brother, son, worker, and societal contributor.

Now, let us examine Freemasonry and how its teaching addresses life's daily challenges. Robert is 40 years old and has struggled with his weight. Starting at age 37, he gained ten pounds each year, which has become a primary concern. After visiting his physician, his metabolism has slowed due to age, a poor diet, lack of exercise, restless sleep, stress, and long work hours.

Robert's physician prescribed a healthier lifestyle to prevent obesity, high blood pressure, stroke, heart attack, sleep apnea, and the need for medication. This included a balanced diet, exercise, sufficient sleep, vacation time, spending more time with family and friends, meditation, or spiritual pursuit, choosing a hobby, and regular check-ups to monitor his progress.

Similarly, in Freemasonry, the twenty-four-inch gauge symbolizes the importance of a balanced lifestyle. As the twenty-four-inch gauge represents balance in speculative Masonry, living a balanced lifestyle is crucial for our physical and mental well-being in the short and long term.

## Weekly Guide

**Define Word**: Freemasonry is a beautiful/peculiar system of morality veiled in allegory and illustrated with/by symbols.

**Life Situation**: Robert is 40 years old. From age 37, he has gained ten pounds a year, becoming a real problem.

**Strength**: Robert's physician placed him on a healthier lifestyle, including a workout regime, eating healthier, proper sleep, vacations, family time, meditation, spirituality, choosing a hobby, and monthly checks to monitor his progress.

**Weakness**: Robert's metabolism slowed due to aging, a poor diet, lack of exercise, restless sleep, stress, and working longer hours, all contributing to his weight gain.

**Freemasonry**: The twenty-four-inch gauge by operative masons is a tool. Speculative Masons use the twenty-four-inch gauge as a symbol to illustrate the importance of a balanced lifestyle.

# Chapter 5
# Masonic Words

Masonic words seem archaic. However, these words are essential to genuinely understand Freemasonry's beauty and truths. Words can be both beautiful and ugly, depending on their literal meanings, sound, appearance, and usage, and can sometimes be highly deceiving.

Masons, when performing degrees, studying ancient charges, doing research papers, or reading literature, sometimes come across words they do not know or what they mean. Becoming familiar with Masonic terms will help increase your vocabulary and help you understand words associated with Freemasonry.

While studying for the Master Mason degree, the Worshipful Master encountered some unfamiliar terminology. Two words were "unfeigned" and "pilasters." After reading Words of Freemasonry: A Weekly Guide to Self-Improvement, he learned how to pronounce these words and their definitions through research and practice, which helped perform the Master Mason lecturer.

## Masonic Words

| | |
|---|---|
| Ardor: | The fiery intensity of feeling. |
| Admonish: | To counsel another person gently and constructively. |
| Allegory | A literary style that uses symbols, characters, or events to represent an abstract idea suggestively. |
| Allude | A hint. Make a disguised reference about a person, place, or thing. |
| Archaic | Out of use. As extremely old as it seems to belong to an earlier period. |
| Aspersion | An unfavorable or damaging remark. |
| Barbarous | Lack of refinement or culture. Coarse, very cruel, savage. |
| Benediction | A ceremonial prayer requesting divine protection |
| Beneficent | A benefit. Doing or producing well. |
| Beseech | To earnestly ask our request. |

| Bourne | An archaic term for a goal or destination |
| --- | --- |
| Candor | Candid. The quality of being honest and straightforward in attitude and speech. |
| Celestial | Relating to Heaven or the spirit. |
| Censure | Harsh criticism or disapproval. |
| Circumscribe | To draw a line or a boundary around. |
| Circumspection | Knowing how to avoid embarrassment or distress by being prudent. |
| Conciliates | Compromise- the ability to come to terms in the interest of obtaining goodwill. |
| Conform | The ability to adapt oneself. |
| Consecrated | Solemnly dedicated to or set apart for a high purpose, usually a Holy purpose. |
| Contrive | To come up with (an idea, plan, explanation, theory, or principle) after a mental effort. |

| Convex | Curving or bulging outward. |
|---|---|
| Countenance | Consent to or give permission. |
| Cowans | Profanes, pretenders, intruders, eavesdroppers. Those are seeking to obtain the Masonic words and secrets of Masonry without having been admitted to the fraternity. |
| Delineate | To accurately depict a shape. To draw or trace the outline of; sketch out. |
| Deluge | An overwhelming number or amount of an item, as in a deluge of rain. |
| Demean | To reduce in worth or character. |

| Deportment | A manner of personal conduct or behavior. |
|---|---|
| Derogatory | Implies contempt or disapproval, such as a derogatory remark. |
| Diligent | Taking care, patience, and perseverance in carrying out tasks. |

| | |
|---|---|
| Discerning | Having, revealing, and exercising keen insight and good judgment. |
| Discordant | Conflicting. Not in agreement or harmony. |
| Discreet | Tactful. Good at keeping secrets subtle and unobtrusive. |
| Diurnal | Occurring in the daytime. Belonging to the period of daylight. (This is one of the Masonic words that its meaning few people understand.) |
| Divest | To deprive, remove, or take away possessions from someone. |
| Eavesdropper | One who stands under the eaves or near the window or door of a house to listen; hence, a secret listener. |
| Ecliptic | An astronomic plane containing the Earth's orbit around the Sun. An imaginary line followed on the earth's surface by the direct ray of the Sun during the year. Solomon's temple, located in Jerusalem, is north of this line. |
| Edifice | A building. Especially a large or impressive one. |

| | |
|---|---|
| Emblematic | Serving as a visible symbol for something abstract, e.g., as a crown, is emblematic of royalty. |
| Emulation | To copy. An effort made to imitate another person's actions. |
| Endue | To endow. To provide a quality or trait. |
| Esteem | To regard with respect and consideration. |
| Exalted | Noble. Elevated in rank, character, or status. |
| Exhort | To make an urgent appeal. |
| Expedient | Practical. Most appropriate to a purpose. |
| Fallacy | A false, erroneous, or mistaken idea. |
| Fervency | Feelings of great warmth and intensity. |
| Firmament | The vault or expanse of the heavens; the sky. |
| Fruition | To bear fruit. To fulfill. |

| | |
|---|---|
| Grand Artificer | Deity. Creator of the Universe. Master Architect, God, Allah, YHWH, etc. |
| Homage | Expression of high regard. Showing respect or attesting to the worth or influence of another person. |
| Hypocrisy | Falsely assuming the appearance of virtue or religion. |

| | |
|---|---|
| Immemorial | Extending back or existing beyond the reach of memory, record, or tradition. Example: Time immemorial. |
| Implore | To earnestly call or pray for. |
| Inclemency | Physical severity or harshness (commonly concerning the elements or weather); roughness; storminess; rigor; severe cold, wind, rain, or snow. |
| Inculcated | To be taught. To implant by repeated statement or admonition; teach persistently and earnestly. |
| Incumbent | Obligatory. A duty which one is obliged to perform. |

| Indissoluble | Firm, Stable. Incapable of being dissolved, decomposed, or destroyed. |
| --- | --- |
| Ineffable | Not to be spoken because of its sacredness. Unutterable: such as the ineffable name of the Deity. |
| Insidious | Stealthily treacherous or deceitful |
| Inundation | To overwhelm. To flood. |
| Invoking | To call for aid or protection; to invite earnestly or solemnly; to summon; to address in prayer; to solicit or demand by invocation; to implore; as, to invoke the Supreme Being, or to invoke (appeal for) His blessing. |
| Laudable | Deserving commendation; praiseworthy. |
| Licentious | Illegal or Immoral. Disregarding rules. |
| Manifold | A whole entity that is composed of many diverse elements. Example: Manifold destiny. |
| Mercenary | Motivated solely by a desire for monetary or material gain. |

| | |
|---|---|
| Meridian | The position of the sun at noon. |
| Monitorial | Method of mutual instruction. |
| Nicety | Detail, exactness, or precision. |
| Obdurate | Hard, firm, unbending, inflexible, unyielding, stubborn. |
| Oppress | To impose excessive burdens upon; to overload; hence, to treat with unjust rigor. |
| Palliate | To try to mitigate, lessen, cover for, or conceal the gravity of (an offense) by excuses, apologies, etc. |
| Patronize | Regularly attend. |
| Pervade | Permeate, diffuse. To spread through. |
| Pilasters | An ornamental and structural column usually projects about a third of its width from the wall to which it is attached and contains a base and a capital (ornamental piece) on top. A pilaster is part of a wall, whereas a column is freestanding. |

| | |
|---|---|
| Pious | Reverence. Having or showing strong religious feelings and devotion toward the Creator. |

| | |
|---|---|
| Precepts | A rule or principle prescribing a particular course of action or conduct. |
| Prone | Lying flat. Prostrate. |
| Prudent | Wise in handling practical matters, exercising good judgment or common sense.<br><br>Careful regarding one's interests; provident.<br><br>Careful about one's conduct; circumspect. |
| Prudential | Wise. Exercising good judgment and common sense. |
| Recapitulate | Summary. To repeat in a concise form. Short form. Recap. |
| Rectitude | Rightness. Correctness of conduct and principle. |
| Reformation | Improvement. Betterment. Correction of an imperfect state. Reform. |

| Reign | Rule. To have control or influence over. |
|---|---|
| Reprehend | Reprimand. Disapprove. |
| Reverential | Honor, Esteem, Revere, Adore. A feeling or attitude of deep respect tinged with awe. |
| Salutary | Wholesome. Promoting or conducive to some beneficial purpose. A purpose that deserves a salute. |
| Seraphic | A pure, angelic, and burning love or ardor. A Seraphim is one of a class of celestial beings with six wings. Some believe they are the first of the nine classes of angels.<br><br>They are mentioned in the Old Testament in Isaiah. 6:2, 3, 6, 7. Seraph means "fiery ones," an allusion, it is supposed, to their burning love. They are represented as "standing," "hovering?" Above the King as he sat upon his throne, ready at once to minister unto him. Their form appears to have been human, with the addition of their three sets of wings. |

| | |
|---|---|
| Shewbread | Showbread. 1 Sam. 21:1-6. This bread consisted of twelve loaves made of the finest flour. They were flat and thin and were placed in two rows of six each on a table in the holy place before the Lord. They were renewed every Sabbath (Lev. 24:5-9), and those that were removed to give place to the new ones were to be eaten by the priests only in the holy place (see 1 Sam. 21:3-6; comp. Matt. 12:3, 4). The number of the loaves represented the twelve tribes of Israel and the entire spiritual Israel, "the true Israel," and placing them on the table symbolized the entire consecration of Israel to the Lord and their acceptance of God as their God. The table for the bread was made of acacia wood, 3 feet long, 18 inches broad, and 2 feet 3 inches high. It was plated with pure gold. Two staves, plated with gold, passed through golden rings, and were used for carrying them. |
| Shewed | Showed—an archaic word meaning to show, display, or exhibit. |
| Solicit | Request. To petition for something which is desired. |

| | |
|---|---|
| Sublime | Ultimate. The greatest or most supreme and elevated degree. Awe-inspiring. Exalted. |
| Subservient | Useful. Serving or acting in a subordinate capacity through a sense of duty. Compliant and obedient to authority because of a deep understanding of the whole. |
| Subsisted | To Exist. To Be. |
| Sundry | Various and Diverse. Many. |
| Superficies | Superficial. Outward appearance. Shallow. Without depth. Residing on a single plane. |
| Superfluities | Excesses. That which is not needed. |
| Sustenance | Nourishment. That is needed to sustain life. |
| Symmetry | Beauty is a result of balance and a harmonious arrangement. The excellence of proportion. Regularity of form or arrangement in terms of like, reciprocal, or corresponding parts. |
| Synonymous | Same. Similar. Expressing or implying the same idea. |

| Tabernacle | A place of worship. Shelter. A temporary dwelling places. |
| --- | --- |

| | |
| --- | --- |
| Temperate | Moderate. Not extreme in behavior. |
| Tempest | Violent disturbances such as storms or tornados. |
| Temporal | Temporary. For a limited time. |
| Tenets | Principles. |
| Tessellated | Checkered. About or like mosaic tiling. The word "tessellate" means small Square. |
| Unbiased | Fair and impartial. Without bias. |
| Unfeigned | Real. Sincere. Unfaked. |
| Unsullied | Pure. Honorable. Clean. Untainted. |
| Venerable | Extremely old. Worthy of Respect. |
| Vertex | The highest point of something. The point of intersection of lines or the point opposite the base of a figure, as the top point of a triangle or a mountain. |

| Vicissitudes | Changes. Fluctuations. Variations. |
|---|---|
| Vouchsafe | To promise or agree condescendingly because it is in your power. To bestow a special favor. To vouch as safe. |
| Waft | Cause to move to and from. |
| Wrought | Created. Made. Designed. |
| Zeal | With passion. Fervor. An eager and ardent interest in the pursuit of something. [1] |

---

[1] Masonic Lodge of Education Masonic Ritual Words in

## Weekly Guide

**Define Word:**

**Life Situation:**

**Strength:**

**Weakness:**

**Freemasonry:**

# Chapter 6
# Morality

(Kumar, 2008) In the article" Morality and Freemasonry," he describes how the Masonic education system teaches morality to its members in an unusual way, in its ritual and the course of the degree work. It is defined in Masonic ritual as a peculiar system of morality that has existed for several hundred years and remains the central feature of Freemasonry today. The old Chinese adage states, "A journey of a thousand miles begins with the first step," and so be it for our Masonic study of morality. Morality is from the Latin word "moralities," which means manner, character, or proper behavior.

A few months after becoming a Master Mason, I was severely tested by an incident that occurred in my daily life. My father, brother, and I were at my campsite for a relaxing and fun weekend. My dog Sadie, a German shepherd, had been by my side all day on Saturday without a leash. During that afternoon, people had driven past our campsite in golf carts, and she had only attempted to pay attention to them that fateful moment when a golf cart came by faster than usual. Sadie ran out to the golf cart. The gentleman driving that golf cart had no idea she would run out, as I had no idea she would, either. But Sadie did, and the golf cart almost ran her over. I immediately stood up, filled with anger. How dare that guy fly through here on his golf cart and almost run over my dog! I was ready to fight.

Then, my consciousness of those high moral standards as a Freemason kicked in. I immediately thought of the First-Degree Catechism that teaches us, as Masons, to be better people. While standing there, I realized the gentleman on the golf cart was not the only person at fault in this incident; I was also at fault. I immediately walked to the porch of my campsite and retrieved Sadie's leash. By that time, my temper had settled down, and my brother had my dog, Sadie. Sadie was fine and unhurt, and the gentleman on the golf cart apologized as much as I did for the incident. All was well; no one was hurt, and I was a better person and a better Freemason for the learning experience. As a newly made Master Mason, I had just received an authentic life experience.

Looking back on this incident, I was, and I am enormously proud of my actions that day. An incident I experienced tested me and made me angry to the point of wanting to fight. I reacted as a good Master Mason should. I was presented with an incident and used my Compasses as I should have. At this point in my life, I realized I was a Master Mason and in control of my actions.

I often relate this story to the newly Entered Apprentice, friends, and brothers. I am still humble, not knowing when I will be tried again by the outside world. Hopefully, I can reflect upon the training and working tools I have been given as a Master Mason. I must respond appropriately to the incident presented and with those high moral standards based on the training I received from my Lodge and our Fraternity. I am just a reflection of my lodge, am I not?"

The word peculiar used to define Freemasonry is not used in a sense to mean odd but in its beauty and more original connotation of an individual. It is interpreted to mean a system of morality that each Mason must come to understand and practice. True morality, in other words, is a science of conduct, and its application is the art requiring great techniques and skills in its practice.

# Weekly Guide

**Define Word:**

**Life Situation:**

**Strength:**

**Weakness:**

**Freemasonry:**

# Chapter 7
# Allegory

An allegory follows the term "the moral of a story." From its definition in Chapter 5 (Masonic Words), an allegory's literary style uses symbols, characters, or events to represent an abstract idea suggestively. Parables are exciting because they convey hidden messages through characters and events. An allegory is a metaphor, a veiled presentation often displayed by exemplary conduct on the part of its principle character.

Hiram Abiff, the Widow's son, is the main character of this allegory presented to all candidates taken from the third degree in Freemasonry. Hiram is the Chief Architect of King Solomon's Temple. The themes of this allegory are the importance of fidelity, integrity, and certainty of death.

Solomon, King of Israel, Hiram King of Tyre, and Hiram Abiff represent Wisdom, Strength, and Beauty, symbolically the three grand pillars of Freemasonry. Collectively, they illustrate all that is good and pure in humanity. They remind us of the perfection each of us should strive to attain as Masons constantly strive to come closer to that state of perfection and to ensure that the world is left a better place when called to that Celestial Lodge from above.

The three ruffians represent ignorance, prejudice, and greed. They are the forces of evil constantly attempting to undo and defeat the forces of good. Once we understand what each character represents, we can interpret their effects on the human condition.

## Weekly Guide

**Define Word:**

**Life Situation:**

**Strength:**

**Weakness:**

**Freemasonry:**

# Chapter 8
# Esoteric vs. Exoteric

The terms "esoteric" and "exoteric" describe the nature of information or knowledge. They are often used in philosophy, religion, and spirituality to distinguish between different forms of understanding.

"Esoteric" refers to knowledge intended for or likely to be understood by only a few with specialized knowledge or interest. It is often considered mysterious or obscure and requires unique insight or understanding to be fully appreciated.

"Exoteric" refers to knowledge intended for or likely to be understood by the public. It is more accessible, straightforward, and easier to understand than esoteric knowledge.

In general, esoteric knowledge is considered more profound than exoteric knowledge but more challenging to grasp and apply. Exoteric knowledge is often seen as less valuable or meaningful than esoteric knowledge but is more widely applicable and useful in everyday life. A classic example of esoteric and exoteric is illustrated by the most identifiable symbol in Freemasonry today, the square and compasses. Speculative Masons used the square and compass as characters to teach morality and conduct (esoteric). Also, the square and compasses were used by ancient Operative Masons as architectural tools (exoteric).

(Newton, 1973) As quoted in his book, The Builders," Masonry grew from a handicraftsmen guild into a universal brotherhood embracing all men of all professions, ethnicities, and religious beliefs. They retained the symbolism of the old Operative Masonry, its languages, its legends, its rituals, and its oral traditions. They no longer build churches but the spiritual temple of humanity. Using the square not to measure the right angles of blocks and stones, but for evening the inequalities of human character, nor the compasses anymore to describe circles on a tracing board, but to draw a circle of goodwill around all mankind" (p.186).

Before becoming a Mason, the square and compasses symbolized someone as a Mason. However, the square and compasses have a new meaning and significance after joining. (Life Situation)

## Weekly Guide

**Define Word:**


**Life Situation:**


**Strength:**


**Weakness:**


**Freemasonry:**

# Chapter 9
# Square

In Freemasonry, the Square teaches lessons of honesty. The notion of being square in your actions implies being honest and fair. The Square symbolizes our ability to use the teachings of fairness in our actions. It is a reminder to deal "squarely" with someone, as we would want them to treat you.

Nita did not feel her husband David was being square with her regarding how often he would be away from home due to his Masonic involvement. To Nita, every Masonic organization David joined meant another night away from home —a fiscal responsibility for being a member. Masons must remember that spirituality, family, and career precede fraternity affiliation.

# Weekly Guide

**Define Word:**

**Life Situation:**

**Strength:**

**Weakness:**

**Freemasonry:**

# Chapter 10
# Compasses

Most of us remember the compasses from our geometry class. In geometry, it is used for drawing perfect circles and arcs, a crucial element of architectural planning. In Speculative Masonry, the compasses symbolize self-restraint and man's ability to reign in his yearnings to live a balanced lifestyle. In Freemasonry, the compasses draw a symbolic boundary line around our desires, avoiding overindulgence or maintaining moderation in a balanced lifestyle.

In Chapter 4, Robert's weight gain started when he turned thirty-seven. His physicians placed him on a healthier lifestyle regime. Here, the compasses are a valuable symbol of avoiding overindulgence. Robert ate at fast food restaurants high in saturated fats at least four times weekly. He drank sugary beverages with every meal. Robert ate pastry every night before bed. After work, he would watch movies until he fell asleep.

Upon his physician's advice, he would have to change his diet by including a variety of fruits and vegetables, consuming primarily whole grains, including low-fat dairy products, and eating a variety of different foods for his protein needs, including fish and lean meats, eggs, beans, and nuts. Drink more water, which boosts energy, helps in weight loss, aids digestion, detoxifies, hydrates the skin, and prevents dehydration.

However, if he did not change his eating habits, it might lead to obesity, diabetes, high blood pressure, strokes, heart attacks, sleep apnea, medication, and premature death.

# Weekly Guide

**Define Word:**

**Life Situation:**

**Strength:**

**Weakness:**

**Freemasonry:**

# Chapter 11
# Entered Apprentice

The Entered Apprentice degree represents re-birth, which afterward resurrects into a better understanding of himself. The Entered Apprentice is a symbol, one of the noblest in the whole symbolic system of the craft. It represents youth. But beyond that, it means a willingness to submit to discipline and to seek knowledge.

The Entered Apprentice is viewed as a youth groping in moral and mental darkness and seeking enlightenment to guide his steps and point him on a path of fulfillment towards God, humanity, and self-improvement.

Ali Shabazz El was having difficulty learning the Entered Apprentice degree. He needed to be advancing like others in his group. He eventually gave up and did not return. Every new member was assigned a mentor before studying the Entered Apprentice degree. Brother John, a Past Master at Anywhere Lodge, was assigned to Ali to monitor his progress and answer questions or concerns.

After several conversations, John discovered Ali learned better in one-on-one sessions. John and Ali began study sessions, resulting in Ali passing the

Entered Apprentice proficiency exam. From a boost in confidence, Ali rejoined the group and eagerly awaited the upcoming Fellow Craft degree.

## Weekly Guide

**Define Word:**

**Life Situation:**

**Strength:**

**Weakness:**

**Freemasonry:**

# Chapter 12
# Fellow Craft

The Fellow Craft degree represents transitioning from an Entered Apprentice (youth) to adulthood (Fellow Craft). Education and moral character are further refined to prepare a candidate for more enlightenment. In this stage, the goal is to acquire knowledge and character to improve society.

Some key symbols and teachings of the Fellow Craft degree include the building of King Solomon's Temple, the working tools of a Fellow Craft, and lessons of the Middle Chamber. The Fellow Craft degree is an essential process in Mason's journey and instills the values of brotherhood, charity, and the pursuit of excellence.

Education and moral character are further refined to prepare a candidate for more enlightenment. In this stage, the goal is to acquire knowledge and character to improve society.

Mark's college advisor discussed that his first two semesters would include Liberal Arts courses. These courses are geared towards developing strong critical thinking, problem-solving, and communication skills.

# Weekly Guide

**Define Word:**

**Life Situation:**

**Strength:**

**Weakness:**

**Freemasonry:**

# Chapter 13
# Master Mason

The Master Mason degree reflects old age, death, resurrection, and everlasting life. As a Master Mason, you are encouraged to reflect on your deeds and make peace with God because one never knows when the end is near. A man's mortality and legacy are highly stressed in this degree. I want to change, and instead of using a real-life situation, I think a poem from "The Old Master's Wage" (McEvoy, 2011) sums up what a Master Mason should strive to be.

## The Old Master's Wages

I met a dear older man today.
Who wore a Masonic pin.
It was old and faded like the man.
Its edges are worn and thin.

I approached the park bench where he sat,
To give the old brother his due.
I said, "I see you've traveled East,"
He said, "I have, have you?"

I said I had and in my day.
Before the all-seeing sun.
I played in the rubble.
With Jubala, Jubelo, and Jubalum.

He said, "don't laugh at the work, my son."

49

It's good, sweet, and faithful.
And if you've traveled as you said,
It would be best if you gave these things their due.

The word, the sign, the token,
The sweet Masonic prayer.
The vow that you have taken
You have climbed the inner stairs.

The wages of a Mason are never paid in gold.
But the gain comes from contentment.
When you're weak and growing old.

You see, I have carried my obligations
For almost 50 years.
It has helped me through the hardships
And the failures full of tears.

Now, I'm losing my mind and body.
Death is near, but I don't despair.
I've lived my life on the level
And I'm dying on the Square.

Sometimes, the greatest lessons
Are those that are learned anew
And the older man in the park today
Has changed my point of view.

To all my Masonic brothers
The only secret is to care.
May you live on the level
And part upon the Square.

**By Neil Neddermeyer**

# Weekly Guide

**Define Word:**


**Life Situation:**


**Strength:**


**Weakness:**


**Freemasonry:**

# Chapter 14
# The Volume of Scared Law

The Volume of Sacred Law (VSL) is a Masonic term used for whatever religious or Book of Law is displayed at the altar. It is an essential part of the obligation in each degree. It works because the book has meaning and is sacred to the individual taking the oath. But what if a man is not a Christian and the Bible has no meaning? That is why it is called The Volume of Sacred Law; whichever book is held sacred to a person is used. In Christian countries, it is the Holy Bible. Lodges in other countries have the religious book of their predominant religion at the altar as their Volume of Sacred Law.

One of the beauties of Masonry is its tolerance for any religion that acknowledges a Deity. Freemasonry accepts men of different faiths and accommodates them with their sacred books at the altar.

I remember visiting the Grand Lodge of New York, and the lodge I attended had all three Volumes of Sacred Law at the altar: The Holy Bible, The Holy Quran, and The Torah.

## Weekly Guide

**Define Word:**

**Life Situation:**

**Strength:**

**Weakness:**

**Freemasonry:**

# Chapter 15
# Level

The level is a symbol of equality. The equality expressed here does not mean wealth or social distinction. When someone in Freemasonry is on the level, they are honest and deal with someone fairly. In the eyes of death, it is often referred to in Masonry as the Great Leveler. It means death comes for all, no matter what station we have attained. It reminds Freemasons that no matter what we do inside the fraternity or what position we hold or held; we have a responsibility to our fellow men to treat each other as equals.

As the lodge ends, the Worshipful Master assembles all members in attendance to the floor, showing a sign of unity, and they are all on the same level. It symbolizes they are standing together equally, and no one is exempt from standing shoulder to shoulder with their brothers, no matter their position in life. As they exit the lodge, the Worshipful Master reminds them that every person they encounter should be treated with the same kindness and honesty as displayed to their lodge brothers.

# Weekly Guide

**Define Word:**

**Life Situation:**

**Strength:**

**Weakness:**

**Freemasonry:**

# Chapter 16
# Plumb

Ancient Operative Masons used the plumb or plumb line to determine if objects were placed perpendicularly. But as Speculative Masons, we are admonished to use the plumb symbolically to judge our actions with humanity and whether they are correctly founded.

Dave found his life spiraling out of control from infidelity, leading to his divorce of twenty-five (25) years and increased drug and alcohol use. As a result, Dave had to enter a drug rehabilitation program to retain his employment. While in recovery, Dave realized he had never been upright or sincere with anyone, not even him. He finally realized he had to treat people the way he wanted to be treated.

## Weekly Guide

**Define Word:**

**Life Situation:**

**Strength:**

**Weakness:**

**Freemasonry:**

# Chapter 17
# Wisdom, Strength, and Beauty

What do Wisdom, Strength, and Beauty mean in Freemasonry? There are so many meanings for Wisdom, Strength, and Beauty; I could author another book on these three words alone. However, we will start with the universe as the temple of deity. Wisdom is to contrive, Strength to support, and Beauty to adorn—Wisdom to conduct all our undertakings—strength to support us in our difficulties, and Beauty to adorn, which starts from within.

At the Lodge, the three principal officers recite the following. The Junior Warden is the beauty and glory of the day. The Senior Warden brings peace and harmony, the strength and support of all institutions, especially ours. The Worshipful Master gives the craft the necessary wisdom and good instructions to pursue their labors.

# Weekly Guide

**Define Word:**

**Life Situation:**

**Strength:**

**Weakness:**

**Freemasonry:**

# Chapter 18
# Fortitude Prudence Temperance and Justice

Fortitude, Prudence, Temperance, and Justice are known as the Four Cardinal Virtues, a concept in ancient Greek philosophy and Catholic theology. Fortitude is courage, the ability to confront fear, danger, or adversity and stand up for one's beliefs. Prudence refers to making wise and practical decisions based on the situation. Temperance, as self-control, involves moderation and self-discipline in all aspects of life, including food, drink, sexual desire, and other bodily appetites. Justice refers to fairness and observance of moral, ethical, and legal obligations. It involves giving people what they are due, such as rendering each person their rights and what is just for them.

These Four Cardinal Virtues are seen as the foundation of a virtuous life and have been influential concepts in Western culture for thousands of years.

Arturo had difficulty deciding whether to marry his long-term girlfriend of twenty years, Beatriz. She gave him an ultimatum that she wanted to get married and raise a family, and if this was not something he wanted to do within the next year, it was over between them.

They have dated since high school. Arturo was the only man Beatriz ever dated. Arturo could have been more faithful; he had several other encounters in the past. Like all relationships, they had problems but seemed to work them out over time.

## Weekly Guide

**Define Word:**

**Life Situation:**

**Strength:**

**Weakness:**

**Freemasonry:**

# Chapter 19
# Brotherly Love, Relief, and Truth

The principle tenets of Freemasonry are – Brotherly Love, Relief, and Truth. Brotherly Love is the practice of treating people the way you want to be treated. Relief embodies charity for all mankind. Truth is honesty and opportunity.

Karter needed help when applying these principle tenets of Freemasonry. As a father, teaching his daughter to respect others in a society of sexual abuse, discrimination, and economic inequality was incredibly challenging.

Being Director of Human Resources for a Fortune 50 Company and striving to bring integrity and professionalism to the workplace was no small task for him and his team. Karter considered himself fair and just when faced with challenging issues, and being truthful and honest with others was not always easy.

## Weekly Guide

**Define Word:**

**Life Situation:**

**Strength:**

**Weakness:**

**Freemasonry:**

# Chapter 20
# Obligation

In Freemasonry, the Masonic obligation is the mystic tie that unites men universally to oaths, solemn promises, agreements, and covenants to God and man. The obligation is a voluntary pledge each Mason takes, which they accept and swear to live by as responsible fraternity members.

Yung Lee became a Master Mason while an international student in the United States. He realized the Masonic brotherhood after becoming an international consultant. While doing business in several foreign countries, he met several masons while visiting lodges. They always assisted, aided, and accommodated him in his travels.

## Weekly Guide

**Define Word:**

**Life Situation:**

**Strength:**

**Weakness:**

**Freemasonry:**

# Chapter 21
# Prayer

Prayer is a submission to God. Prayer is described as a spiritual communion, a supplication, thanksgiving, adoration, or confession to the greatness of the Supreme Architect of the Universe.

Anywhere, Lodge invites guests who might have questions about Freemasonry and are also interested in becoming a Mason to a Lodge Hall meeting. John, a guest, asked if Freemasonry was not a religion, why Masons pray at meetings, and to what God?

Worshipful Master Clarke Hill addressed the questions in this matter. Freemasonry has never been considered a religion nor a substitute for religion. The only requirement of Masons is a belief in God as part of its membership and advocates no sectarian faith or practice. Masonic ceremonies include traditional prayers to reaffirm everyone's dependence on God. Also, Masons are taught to seek reverence from the Supreme Architect of the Universe. Freemasonry teaches tolerance, but Masonic meetings do not discuss religion and politics.

## Weekly Guide

**Define Word:**


**Life Situation:**


**Strength:**


**Weakness:**


**Freemasonry:**

# Chapter 22
# The Letter "G"

The letter "G" is a symbol with many interpretations, depending on the context. One of the most common interpretations is geometry, which is considered the foundation of the craft and a vital component of the teachings. It is also one of the seven liberal arts and sciences in which Freemasons have historically been interested.

Another interpretation of the letter "G" is that it stands for "God" and symbolizes a belief in the Supreme Being. In some lodges and jurisdictions, the letter "G" stands for "Grand Architect of the Universe," acknowledging the faith in a guiding intelligence behind the creation and ordering of the cosmos.

Regardless of the interpretation, the letter "G" is an essential symbol in Freemasonry and is often incorporated into lodge halls and other Masonic spaces. Adding the letter" G" to the square and compasses is a topic of debate, and there is no definitive answer as to when it was used.

In a lecture by Carlos Moses, he stated," It is worth noting that not all Masonic jurisdictions use the letter G in the center of the square and compasses. The use of symbols and emblems in Freemasonry varies across different traditions and regions, and their meanings may also differ. However, it is accepted that the letter "G" was added to the emblem sometime in the 18th century in the United States.[2]

---

[2] Coil, H. W. (1961). *Coils Masonic Encyclopedia*. New York, New York, Macoy Publishing and Masonic Supply Company

# Weekly Guide

**Define Word:**

**Life Situation:**

**Strength:**

**Weakness:**

**Freemasonry:**

# Chapter 23
# 47<sup>th</sup> Problem of Euclid

The 47th Problem of Euclid, also known as Euclid's Proposition 47 or Pythagorean Theorem, is a mathematical theorem. In Freemasonry, the 47th Problem of Euclid is used as a symbol of a connection between mathematical knowledge and the principles of the fraternity. The Pythagorean Theorem is said to represent the concept of balance and proportion in both mathematics and life. It also symbolizes physical and moral laws have a common origin and can be seen as aspects of universal truth. In Freemasonry, the theorem is often depicted in various symbolic forms and is used to teach lessons about the importance of balance and harmony in one's personal and professional life.

Larry had a real problem with the relation between the 47th Problem of Euclid and Freemasonry. His research discovered that the connection between the Pythagorean Theorem and Freemasonry is sometimes accepted as a matter of interpretation and tradition within the craft. There are varying opinions and interpretations of the significance of this mathematical principle within the Masonic ritual; not all Masons may view it similarly.

# Weekly Guide

**Define Word:**

**Life Situation:**

**Strength:**

**Weakness:**

**Freemasonry:**

# Chapter 24
# The All-Seeing Eye

The All-Seeing Eye is associated with Freemasonry. In Freemasonry, the All-Seeing Eye is the omniscience of God, who is believed to watch over and protect all humanity. In Freemasonry iconography, the All-Seeing Eye is a single eye surrounded by light rays and sometimes floating above a pyramid. The pyramid symbolizes strength and stability and is thought to represent the idea of a secure foundation for moral and ethical principles.

While the All-Seeing Eye is a common symbol in Freemasonry, its interpretation and significance may vary depending on the Masonic jurisdiction. Nevertheless, it is considered a symbol of divine watchfulness that guides all people's actions and helps ensure they follow moral and ethical principles.

The conspiracy theorist would have the public believe that the All-Seeing Eye shown above the unfinished pyramid indicates the influence of Freemasonry in the United States. However, Masonic use of the All-Seeing Eye dates back 14 years after the Great Seal. Furthermore, Benjamin Franklin was the only Mason among the various design committees. Whose seal was not adopted? Likewise, various Masonic organizations have explicitly denied connection to the seal's connection.

# Weekly Guide

**Define Word:**

**Life Situation:**

**Strength:**

**Weakness:**

**Freemasonry:**

# Chapter 25
# Operative Masonry

Masonry is understood under two denominations: Operative and Speculative. Operative means having the ability to function and have an effect. Operative Masonry was a trade organization of stonemasons who built structures such as castles and cathedrals in the Middle Ages. Speculative Masonry emerged after a period of Operative Masonry during the late 17th and early 18th centuries, as the demand for skilled stonemasons decreased with the shift from Gothic architecture to Renaissance styles.

During this time, members of the stonemason guilds (Free) began to admit non-stonemasons as members (Accepted) interested in the moral, ethical, and spiritual teachings that were part of the guild's traditions and ceremonies. It marked the beginning of Speculative Masonry, where the interest shifted from the practical aspects of stonemasonry to the symbolic and philosophical elements.

Chris, a newly raised brother, was appointed Junior Steward of his Lodge. In the upcoming degree, he was assigned to deliver the working tools in the Entered Apprentice degree, which outlines the meaning of Operative and Speculative Masonry and the practical and symbolic meanings of both the twenty-four-inch gauge and the common gavel. His deliverance was flawless.

## Weekly Guide

**Define Word:**

**Life Situation:**

**Strength:**

**Weakness:**

**Freemasonry:**

# Chapter 26
# Speculative Masonry

Speculative means to engage in, express, or based on conjecture rather than knowledge. Speculative Masonry uses the tools and skills of Operative Masons as metaphors for living a good life. Speculative Freemasonry, also known as "Accepted," means providing Masons with opportunities to improve their lives through teaching Freemasonry. Speculative Freemasonry is the application of Operative Freemasonry's principles for moral and intellectual development.

So, instead of using tools to build physical structures, they speculated on how to use these same tools symbolically to build, improve, and strengthen the character of an individual man. Through self-improvement, Speculative Masons learned to make a moral character, engage in personal development, enlighten themselves in education, and get inspired by spirituality and a feeling of charity or goodwill toward all mankind.

Javier, a historian, traced back Speculative Masonry, incorporating other philosophies such as the Knights Templar, the tradition of "Hermeticism," and Alchemy. Speculative Masons brought with them a desire to explore the symbolic and philosophical aspects of the craft and to use the tools and symbols of stonemasonry as allegories for moral and ethical lessons known to many as the Enlightenment Age.

# Weekly Guide

**Define Word:**

**Life Situation:**

**Strength:**

**Weakness:**

**Freemasonry**

# Chapter 27
# Rough and Perfect Ashlar

The Rough Ashlar symbolizes the individual before their initiation into the Fraternity. It is typically depicted as a rough, unshaped block of stone, representing the rude and uncultivated nature of the individual before they begin their journey of self-improvement through the teachings of Freemasonry.

In Masonic lodges, the Rough Ashlar is often placed alongside the Perfect Ashlar, a symbol of the perfected, enlightened individual who has undergone the transformative initiation process. The two signs inform members of the importance of continuous self-improvement and personal growth. It further emphasizes the idea of the Rough Ashlar representing the unfinished and imperfect individual, who must work to become more like the Perfect Ashlar, just as rough stones are polished to become part of the structure of a great building.

In Freemasonry, the Perfect Ashlar is a symbol that represents the ideal of perfection and completion in Mason's life and work. It is a smooth, precisely cut stone that is a standard comparison for the Rough Ashlar. It is an uncut stone that symbolizes the imperfections and rough edges in Mason's character that he seeks to smooth out through his personal and spiritual growth.

The Perfect Ashlar is the goal of Mason's journey, representing the highest moral, ethical, and spiritual development he can attain. It serves as a reminder that Masons should continually strive to improve themselves and their communities and to build their lives upon the foundation of wisdom, strength, and beauty. In general, the Perfect Ashlar symbolizes the idea that people can and should continuously strive to improve themselves and their lives, seeking to achieve their full potential and live according to their highest ideals.

Tommy McGee, a Past Master of Anywhere Lodge. Every year, he invited his family to the open installation of officers. One year in particular, his youngest daughter, Sara, asked why stones of different shapes were placed in front of the lodge. Although it was briefly discussed by the installing officer that evening, Tommy explained the meaning behind the Rough and Perfect Ashlar to his daughter.

## Weekly Guide

**Define Word:**


**Life Situation:**


**Strength:**


**Weakness:**


**Freemasonry:**

# Chapter 28
# Chamber of Reflection

The Chamber of Reflection is a room in some lodges. It is meant to serve as a place where a Freemason can go to reflect on the events of the day, meditate on the principles of the fraternity, and contemplate the obligations they have taken upon themselves as a member of the organization.

The Chamber of Reflection is usually a small, quiet, sparsely furnished, decorated room. The furnishings may include a small altar, a mirror, and sometimes a representation of the All-Seeing Eye. The room is meant to be a place for contemplation and introspection. It is intended to help Freemasons reflect on the moral and ethical lessons they have learned as members of the organization.

In some lodges, the Chamber of Reflection may also be used as part of the initiation ceremony, where candidates reflect on their motivations for seeking membership in the fraternity and consider the obligations, they will assume upon being initiated.

The Chamber of Reflection is an integral part of the symbolic architecture of Freemasonry. It serves as a standard for the moral and ethical principles at the core of the organization's teachings.

Dan Brown introduces the reader to The Lost Symbol, a fictional thriller involving the Freemason's most excellent initiatory tool – the Chamber of Reflection. "The skull sat atop a rickety wooden desk against the chamber's rear wall. Two human leg bones sat beside the skull, along with a collection of other items meticulously arranged on the desk in a shrine-like fashion – an antique hourglass, a crystal flask, a candle, two saucers of pale powder, and a sheet of paper. Staged against the wall stood a fearsome long scythe, its curved blade as familiar as the Grim Reaper. 'This room is Masonic.' Sato demanded, turning from the skull, and staring at Langdon in the darkness."

Langdon nodded calmly, 'It is called a Chamber of Reflection. These rooms are designed as cold, austere places where a Mason can reflect on his mortality. By meditating on the inevitability of death, Masons reflects on the fleeting nature of life.'

## Weekly Guide

**Define Word:**

**Life Situation:**

**Strength:**

**Weakness:**

**Freemasonry:**

# Chapter 29
# King Solomon's Temple

Freemasons are committed to a life of self-improvement. Philosophy uses symbolic working tools to seek an understanding and reflect deeply on ways to improve the world. The principle tenants of Brotherly Love, Relief, and Truth are the cornerstones of the fraternity; the building of King Solomon's Temple represents the path of personal development as they journey through as Masons. Biblical narratives, historical documentation, and lectures provide insight into the symbolism of King Solomon's Temple and how it relates to Freemasonry today. Let us learn from the history and valuable symbolism taught by the craft.

Beyond any religious context, building this unique structure provides a symbolic foundation for self-improvement in Freemasonry. Masonic tradition and ritual refer to the physical architectural processes of the temple's creation as enlightenment and self-growth. King Solomon's Temple depicts the capabilities of men working collaboratively, using the right tools to improve themselves for the world.

Many archaeologists have hunted for evidence to support or refute the ancient Biblical stories about Israel. But the First Temple in Jerusalem, King Sol-

omon's Temple, and its builder, King Solomon, remain a mystery.

## Weekly Guide

**Define Word:**

**Life Situation:**

**Strength:**

**Weakness:**

**Freemasonry:**

# Chapter 30
# Blue Lodge

The Bible emphasizes blue as a color, symbolizing goodness, and immortality. The Blue Lodge has been here in America from the beginning of Freemasonry on the shores, and the term "Blue Lodge" has become widely used. Initially, it was frowned upon, and lodges were called Craft Lodges or Ancient Craft Lodges. Some were even called St. Johns Lodge. Masonic scholars had mixed opinions when blue first came to be associated with Freemasonry, although some historians think that initially, the color was used in craft masonry to represent the sky; blue represents a peculiar characteristic of a Master Mason. The Blue Lodge has three Masonic degrees conferred: The Entered Apprentice, The Fellow Craft, and The Master Mason degree.

In curiosity, Gary asked why the Lodge he belonged to was called a "Blue Lodge" and not just called Anywhere Lodge. He asked every brother, and everyone had a different answer, which confused him. Gary concluded it is all about one's interpretation from the many lecturers, degrees, and discussions of why it is known as a Blue Lodge.

# Weekly Guide

**Define Word:**

**Life Situation:**

**Strength:**

**Weakness:**

**Freemasonry:**

# Chapter 31
# Clandestine Masonry

Clandestine means secret or hidden. The French word "clandestine" is defined as "done in a hiding place made secretly and against laws," which better suits the Masonic definition as illegal, not authorized. In some jurisdictions, they are called irregular, a deviation from custom.

Clandestine Masonry is a body of bogus members forming a lodge without the recognized Grand Lodge's consent or continuing to work after its charter has been revoked. Masons governed by duly constituted Grand Lodges are forbidden to associate or converse in Masonic subjects with clandestine or irregulars.

At one time, Jamal was a clandestine Mason who wanted to know the truth. He reached out to his Grand Master at the time for answers. He was honest, noted Jamal. When I asked him about being considered a clandestine mason, he said, "This is the truth. They call us clandestine... they have some nerve. Our protocol was the same process they did in their lodges. Who tells these white guys they can do it and we cannot?" It is common for some clandestine groups to play to the same racial tensions that have historically divided good men in our country since the birth of our democracy.

## Weekly Guide

**Define Word:**

**Life Situation:**

**Strength:**

**Weakness:**

**Freemasonry:**

# Chapter 32
# The Craft

The Craft is another term for Freemasonry. Here, the three Masonic degrees, Entered Apprentice, Fellow Craft, and Master Mason are conferred. After a candidate is raised to the Sublime degree of Master Mason, they are considered to have full membership in the fraternity. The business of Craft Masonry revolves around these three initiation ceremonies. However, there are plenty of other businesses that center around Masonic education and charitable contributions.

Brother Patel was initiated, passed, and raised to the sublime degree of Master Mason.

# Weekly Guide

**Define Word:**

**Life Situation:**

**Strength:**

**Weakness:**

**Freemasonry:**

# Chapter 33
# Faith, Hope, and Charity

Faith, Hope, and Charity are three critical principles in Freemasonry. They represent the moral and ethical values Masons strive to embody daily. Faith refers to the belief in a higher power or Supreme Being. Hope refers to the confidence in a positive outcome or future and the desire to work towards that future. Masons are encouraged to maintain a positive outlook and never give up on adversity. Charity refers to the practice of giving to others in need. Masons are encouraged to be generous and to help those who are less fortunate.

In Freemasonry, these three principles are essential to the development of a well-rounded and virtuous character. By practicing Faith, Hope, and Charity, Masons can build better relationships with others and improve the world around them. The beauty of Freemasonry is the inclusion of all faiths, whether Christian, Jewish, Muslim, Sikh, Hindu, Shinto, Buddhist, Zoroastrian, and so on. In daily life, hardships, fears, and frustrations are abundant; we often encounter obstacles that make life difficult, people we do not like, or those who make us feel unwelcome, but if we have the determination and hope to anchor us towards the right path, we will succeed. Hopefully, our charitable deeds will live forever.

Bill Steiner interprets Faith, Hope, and Charity to be strictly esoteric. Faith, Hope, and Charity, the three greatest forces are Faith, which is the only true wisdom and the very foundation of all humanity; Hope, which is strength and ensures success; and Charity, which is beauty and alone, makes united efforts possible.

# Weekly Guide

**Define Word:**

**Life Situation:**

**Strength:**

**Weakness:**

**Freemasonry:**

# Chapter 34
# Seven Liberal Arts and Sciences

The Seven Liberal Arts and Sciences taught by Freemasonry are grammar, rhetoric, logic, arithmetic, geometry, music, and astronomy. Grammar is the science that leads us to express ideas and correct inappropriate words. Rhetoric is applying language to instruct and persuade the listener or reader. Logic teaches us how to think and reason with propriety. Arithmetic is the science of computing by numbers, which is essential in a thorough knowledge of all mathematical science and a valuable tool in the pursuit of our daily vocations. Geometry is the application of Arithmetic to sensible quantities. It is, of all sciences, the most important as regards Masonry since it enables us to measure and survey the globe we inhabit when our minds and thoughts are enlarged by contemplating all the wonders these sciences open to our view. Music softens our hearts and cultivates our affections through its soothing influences.

In Chapter 12, Fellow Craft, Mark's college advisor, explained his first two semesters would consist of Liberal Arts and Science electives. Again, we see how higher learning uses Liberal Arts and Sciences by encompassing grammar, rhetoric, logic, arithmetic, geometry, music, and astronomy into a general elective curriculum.

## Weekly Guide

**Define Word:**

**Life Situation:**

**Strength:**

**Weakness:**

**Freemasonry:**

# Chapter 35
# Masonic Ritual

Masonic ritual is the heart and soul of Freemasonry. A lodge would be considered another social or charitable organization without Masonic rituals. It binds Masons with each other from time immemorial. Tradition is not simply made up of words. Any individual with access to the internet can obtain a wealth of information about the formalities of rituals. Freemasonry is a beautiful and profound system of morality in its Masonic ritual, veiled in allegories and illustrated with symbols.

Jonathan was amazed at how Masons memorized and performed rituals and how much time went into conferring a degree. He thought afterward, "I could never do that," but was willing to try if it meant becoming a better man.

## Weekly Guide

**Define Word:**

**Life Situation:**

**Strength:**

**Weakness:**

**Freemasonry:**

# Chapter 36
# Point Within the Circle

The Point Within the Circle is a symbol commonly found in about every lodge. It consists of a point or dot within a circle with two perpendicular lines. This symbol has several interpretations within the context of Freemasonry.

According to interpretation, the point represents an individual Mason, the circle represents the boundary of his actions, and the lines intersecting at the point represent the moral compasses that guide his actions. This symbol suggests to Freemasons they should strive to keep their actions within the bounds of morality.

From another interpretation, the circle represents the universe or the world, while the point represents the individual Mason's place. The lines intersecting at this point represent the connection between the individual and the larger universe. Above the Point Within the Circle rest the Volume of the Sacred Law refers to the holy book, religion, or faith followed by a Masonic lodge. The book serves as a source of moral guidance and inspiration for lodge members. These symbols are guidelines for Freemasons to fulfill their duties, strive for morality, and consider their place in the extensive world.

As per tradition, St. John the Baptist corresponds to the summer solstice, while St. John the Evangelist corresponds to the winter solstice. Therefore, these two lines commonly represent summer and winter solstices celebrated as The Feast of John. Regardless of its origin or interpretation, the symbol reminds Freemasons everywhere to remain faithful to their obligations and those around them.

Josh was battling years of depression and had good and bad days. He was taking medication prescribed by his physician. He was advised to research depression, which would help him cope with his disorder. Josh read many articles describing depression as a chronic, disabling lifestyle experience. He learned from research several types of depression ranging from mild, moderate, to severe mood swings. The study that helped him with his depression most was the Point Within the Circle in Freemasonry. He realized the central issue in his life was surrounded by daily challenges, and how he reacted to these circumstances would determine how successful he would be. He also understood that he needed spiritual intervention to strengthen him internally.

## Weekly Guide

**Define Word:**

**Life Situation:**

**Strength:**

**Weakness:**

**Freemasonry:**

# Chapter 37
# Three Distinct Knocks

Three Distinct Knocks alarms the lodge and notifies the Worshipful Master that the candidate is fully prepared for admission. What is gained by a candidate's entrance into a sacred lodge? The candidate is taught the importance of the three. He is reminded that he sought admission through a friend. He is duly and truly prepared by the process he underwent before becoming a Mason. Finally, he desires to receive a part of Freemasonry's rights and benefits.

The Holy Bible King James Version Matthew 7:7 – Ask, and it shall be given you; seek, and ye shall find; knock, and it shall be opened unto you:

Jacob, the Senior Deacon at Anywhere Lodge, listened for the three distinct knocks coming from the enter door of the lodge, notifying the Worshipful Master, Wardens, and brethren the candidate was without prepared for admission.

# Weekly Guide

**Define Word:**

**Life Situation:**

**Strength:**

**Weakness:**

**Freemasonry:**

# Chapter 38
# Of My Own Free Will and Accord

"Of My Own Free Will and Accord" is a phrase every Freemason is acquainted with. It is one of several expressions used in rituals throughout the Masonic world. "Of my own free will and accord" denotes liberty of choice, self-determination, and lack of restraint. At the same time, accord implies whole-heartedness, free from inducement or pressure. Masons use the word "free" in several ways: free will and accord, Freemason, freeborn, accessible, and accepted; these words are frequently used in Freemasonry, and few questions are ever asked about their usage.

Because of his new position at work, Lester had difficulty meeting his commitment as Junior Steward at the lodge. He discussed this situation with the Worshipful Master and was told that his dedication to the lodge was not as essential as his career and that everything he did for his lodge was of his own free will and accord.

# Weekly Guide

**Define Word:**


**Life Situation:**


**Strength:**


**Weakness:**


**Freemasonry:**

# Chapter 39
# Masonic Education

Masonic Education is based on values, history, symbols, and myths. It encompasses lessons in leadership, self-improvement, and community. Masonic education enables members to seek answers to become better men.

Some of the Masonic education consists of:
- Study of history.
- Enhance current leadership skills.
- Delve into philosophy.
- Focus on ritual and symbolism.
- Continual formal education.

Brother Patel was not a ritualist but enjoyed esoteric Masonry. He authored a research paper entitled "The Western Tradition Mystical Schools of Esoteric Philosophy and Its Influence on Freemasonry.

## Weekly Guide

**Define Word:**


**Life Situation:**


**Strength:**


**Weakness:**


**Freemasonry:**

# Chapter 40
# Masonic Leadership

I will keep you from a textbook definition of Masonic Leadership. However, I want to focus on what Masonic Leadership must develop. Not using the dreaded term "change" but more so "evolve." The working population is rapidly developing into shorter working hours or working from home. Membership in organizations outside of work should be growing. Today, Grand Lodge Jurisdictions are finding the opposite: an alarming statistic of declining membership. Many of the brethren are dying. Many more are giving up their Masonic affiliation by refusing to pay their dues, and fewer men are petitioning lodges.

Surprisingly, membership is down across the board in all community-based organizations; the overall situation presents a picture of grave concern to every Masonic leader who realizes no other organization, whether civil or fraternal, has as much to offer its membership as Masonic leadership. What must be done to retain members? Before we start to criticize Worshipful Masters of lodges for allowing their membership to lapse for non-payment of dues (NPD), we should take a long critical observation of Freemasonry as it is being exemplified in lodges today, particularly the leadership in our respective Grand Lodges. In doing so, let us ascertain the reason for our dilemma of suspensions and non-members' lack of interest in the fraternity.

Today's men are more educated than any generation that has preceded them. Younger men are spending their leisure time obtaining vast information at their fingertips. Modern people belong to organizations managed effectively and technologically driven by competent people with leadership skills. With that said, why is the question ever brought up? Why aren't lodges retaining men because, in many cases, they are coming into an inefficiently operated Masonic lodge?

On the flip side, a lodge whose Master and officers are leaders in the true sense of the word, a lodge where brethren are embracing technology, operates efficiently, rituals are exemplified to perfection, value membership retention, has a solid Masonic educational program, mentoring program, youth programs, outreach activities, and community involvement, I will show you a thriving Masonic lodge.

The question concerning Masonic leadership today should be, "Are we still attracting and retaining men with leadership qualities?" I am a firm believer that leadership is a learned skill set. Is the present Masonic leadership providing the necessary skill sets to sustain itself by attracting future leaders? Does the Masonic fraternity have men with leadership ability within its membership? If so, how are they utilizing this asset to uplift their lodges and Grand Lodges and create a positive experience for their membership?

Joel, 45, is married with no children. He has an MBA from an Ivy League University. He loves reading Western philosophy and ancient mystery schools. He minored in philosophy as an undergraduate. In college, he joined a fraternity. He works as a financial analyst for a Fortune 500 company and manages a staff of fifty analysts. His company participates in many community activities. He still attends the church he went to as a child. He played soccer all his life but stopped playing a year ago because of a knee injury. He is a volunteer soccer coach for the girls' high school team in his town.

Joel comes from a family of Masons. His grandfather, father, and uncles were all Masons. His family never discussed becoming a Mason with him, nor did they discuss Masonry at family gatherings, but he wanted to become a Mason.

Joel was finally excited when he petitioned his grandfather and father's lodge. After being raised, the Worshipful Master asked him if he would be an officer in the lodge. He accepted the position of Junior Steward. Upon receiving the position, he was never provided an officer's manual. As Junior Steward, he would cook and prepare meals for the brethren at each lodge meeting. He asked if he could serve on the finance committee, but the lodge bylaws prohibited anyone less than three years in the lodge from being on the finance committee.

At lodge meetings, only minutes were read; nothing educational was provided. Many of the members in the lodge were sixty or older. The lodge had little computer use. The Past Masters saw to the daily operations of the lodge. Under the motto, "This is how it's always been done," Several members served as Worshipful Master at least three times over the years.

However, there were several encouraging things about the lodge:

1. The lodge had over three million dollars in investment.

2. The members were particularly good at Masonic rituals.

3. The lodge owned the building and paid no city taxes due to their 503 C-10 fraternal non-profit status.

4. The lodge had small fixed operational expenses.

Most of their revenue came from dues and two fundraisers every year. After a year of membership, Joel decided not to renew his dues. He wanted nothing to do with the lodge but remained active in his college fraternity, his job community outreach programs, and soccer coaching. Did the lodge fail to make Joel a better man?

## Weekly Guide

**Define Word:**

**Life Situation:**

**Strength:**

**Weakness:**

**Freemasonry:**

# Chapter 41
# Fraternity

Freemasonry is the world's largest and oldest secular fraternal order, crossing all religious boundaries and bringing men together from all countries and sects in peace and harmony. Its members included significant religious figures, kings, and presidents. Freemasonry has various forms worldwide, with a membership estimated in the millions.

However, the Masonic organization has been declining. Many plans have been implemented to curb the tide of accelerating membership decline. The proposed solutions deal only with current membership retention rather than an answer or even recognition and acceptance of the problem.

Based on statistics, Freemasonry has experienced a consistent decrease since 1959, when there were four million members solely in America. In 2020, the figure was reduced by a million. The data indicate Freemasonry is losing an average of 50,000 members annually. While these figures concern the Masonic community, they reflect a broader trend in many other community-based organizations. Church attendance worldwide has experienced significant declines in overall membership.

Gomez finally understood what members of his fraternity meant when they said the beauty of Freemasonry is traveling. As he traveled, he discovered the beauties of Masonry throughout the world. Although the rituals might be slightly different, they exemplify the same teaching: a belief in God, the importance of family, universal fraternal brotherhood, improving humanity, and self-improvement.

# Weekly Guide

**Define Word:**

**Life Situation:**

**Strength:**

**Weakness:**

**Freemasonry:**

# Chapter 42
# Prince Hall

Prince Hall was an African American abolitionist and prominent leader in the early history of Freemasonry in the United States. Born in Barbados, his actual birth is unknown but expected to be around 1735 or 1738; Hall was a free Black man who lived in Boston, Massachusetts. He and other African American men were granted a charter to form the African Lodge from the Grand Lodge of England in 1784. It marked the creation of what is known as Prince Hall Freemasonry, which has a distinct history and organization from other Masonic lodges.

Prince Hall was a prominent figure in the fight against slavery and was involved in efforts to secure civil rights for African Americans. He petitioned the Massachusetts state government for equal treatment and advocated for education and African American military participation in the American Revolution.

Today, Prince Hall Freemasonry is one of the world's largest and oldest African American fraternal organizations in many countries. Prince Hall is remembered as an activist, a pioneer, and an essential figure in African American and Masonic history.

Fatima Jabbar was assigned a research paper for her African American history class. The professor gave her an assignment on Prince Hall, an abolitionist and prominent leader. She was amazed by the history of Prince Hall Freemasonry, a fraternal organization that traces its roots to African American communities in the United States. Fatima discovered the organization operates under several Grand Lodges, each governing several subordinate lodges.

In her research dating back to 2021, there were approximately fifty (50) Prince Hall Grand Lodges in the United States military stations and several other countries, including Canada, the Caribbean, and West Africa. Some of her research revealed that the exact number of Grand Lodges and lodges could vary, as new lodges may be chartered, and others may merge or close. Additionally, Prince Hall Freemasonry is not universally recognized by all mainstream Masonic organizations,

# Weekly Guide

**Define Word:**

**Life Situation:**

**Strength:**

**Weakness:**

**Freemasonry:**

# Chapter 43
# Ancient Landmarks

Ancient Landmarks are rules that govern Grand Lodges and are nonnegotiable precepts in Freemasonry. Although Ancient Landmarks may differ from jurisdictions, such issues of recognition or regularity are set by these Ancient Landmarks. Every Grand Lodge is autonomous, with no governing body exerting authority over the entire craft of Freemasonry. The interpretations of these rules vary, leading to a difference in precepts. However, Ancient Landmarks, regardless of Jurisdiction, contain the same rules and principles governing Freemasonry from time immorally.

The Most Worshipful Big Boss Grand Master of Masons in the State of Anywhere issued an edict stating, "There will be no alcohol consumption before lodge meetings or when degrees are conferred." Many members were upset by this mandate because they sold libation to generate money for their lodges. This edict did not conflict with the twenty-five (25) Ancient Landmarks. Even the Grand Master must obey the Ancient Landmarks of Freemasonry.

# Weekly Guide

**Define Word:**

**Life Situation:**

**Strength:**

**Weakness:**

**Freemasonry:**

# Chapter 44
# Making Good Men Better

Making Good Men Better is a slogan of every Grand Lodge. This statement means not being better than anyone but striving for betterment through self-improvement. Universally known, the Masonic fraternity aims to improve its members through personal development by enhancing the body, mind, and spirit, influenced, and inspired by Masonic teachings and its tenets.

Freemasonry has, from its conception, freed people from ego-centered consciousness. It emphasizes self-improvement, enlightenment, faith in the Deity, devotion to the country, building a strong family, and charitable contributions. All of which is the foundation of making a good man better. In Freemasonry, the members are initiated, passed, and raised, all requiring learning at each phrase.

So, making good men better is considered a never-ending process. From the first day obligated until laying down one's symbolic working tools, self-improvement is the core value of its teaching. Implementing these fraternal tenets is recommended as a daily practice.

Stan McGregor was a 50-year member of Anywhere Lodge. Just days before his return to the Celestial Lodge above, he stood before his brothers at his last meeting. He profoundly stated, yes, I am a member of the world's largest and most honorable fraternity. One believes through brotherly love; we can offer relief to people in need and help make good men better.

Becoming a Mason has been extremely rewarding. After serving God, my marriage of 60 years and family, my career as a police officer, my military service, and my many charitable contributions, Masonry has provided me with a gratifying life filled with great memories and universal brotherly love.

# Weekly Guide

**Define Word:**

**Life Situation:**

**Strength:**

**Weakness:**

**Freemasonry:**

# Chapter 45
# Worshipful Master

The Operative Masons designed many cathedrals and organized themselves into lodges. Every operative lodge elected a Master to head the group and other officers. Several centuries ago, the word "Worshipful" meant "Respected." Operative Masons elected one Master, Mason, and was given the title Worshipful Master, indicating he was a respected worker.

In modern times, Speculative lodges also elect a Worshipful Master every year. The Worshipful Master serves as the Chief Executive Officer of a lodge and presides over all the meetings. The Worshipful Master is in the East of the lodge and conducts all the lodge's business. He is vested with dictatorial powers. He also presides over rituals and ceremonies.

Worshipful Brother Lopez, on the night of the election for Worshipful Master, placed his name as a nominee to run again. The Senior Warden, who many thought did an understanding job, was surprised by this turn of events, which shook all the members. When the final votes were counted, Brother Lopez won by one vote. The outcome shocked fifty percent of the membership, resulting in half of the members demitting and joining other lodges.

## Weekly Guide

**Define Word:**

**Life Situation:**

**Strength:**

**Weakness:**

**Freemasonry:**

# Chapter 46
# Senior Warden

The Senior Warden station is in the West in a Masonic lodge. He is the second in command. He presides over the lodge in the absence of the Worshipful Master. The Senior Warden's jewel is the level. It is a symbol of equality that shall always exist in the lodge. Located at his station is a column that represents strength referred to as Jachin, the right-hand pillar at the door at King Solomon's Temple. The word Warden has many different meanings. Its basic Masonic meaning is overseeing the craft, having supervisory responsibilities, or governing lodge committees, and being well-versed in the lodge bylaws and the Grand Lodge Constitution.

Mark McKey, the Senior Warden of Anywhere Lodge, was a third-generation Mason. Both his grandfather and father were Worshipful Masters of Anywhere Lodge. Brother McKey was proud to follow his family legacy. As the year progressed and closer to the vote and installation, Mark became nervous and questioned his leadership. He pondered the thought of fulfilling his family legacy of being a good Worshipful Master. Could he lead the lodge successfully, and most importantly, did he have the support and confidence of the brethren? All were valid questions only he could answer and fulfill.

# Weekly Guide

**Define Word:**

**Life Situation:**

**Strength:**

**Weakness:**

**Freemasonry:**

# Chapter 47
# Junior Warden

The Junior Warden is an elected position by the brethren in the lodge. He is third in command. His role is compared to a Second Vice-President. The Junior Warden station is in the South of a lodge. Symbolically, its location represents the sun at the meridian. He is responsible for when a lodge is on refreshment and in charge of the Stewards. His jewel is the plumb. It symbolizes proper behavior. Operative Masons used the plumb as a tool for the alignment of a vertical surface.

Sung Yang was elected and installed as Junior Warden of Anywhere Lodge; he was excited and assured the brethren he would work hard to ensure the lodge remained progressing in the right direction. He was exceptionally good at supervising the Stewards in preparing collation and assisting the Worshipful Master and Senior Warden in fundraising events, serving on many lodge committees, and being well-known throughout the district as a good Mason.

However, the one area he needed improvement was the Masonic ritual. Over the years, he has worked hard at becoming efficient in ritual. Before being elected Senior Warden, one of the requirements, Sung Yang would have to confer an Entered Apprentice degree.

# Weekly Guide

**Define Word:**

**Life Situation:**

**Strength:**

**Weakness:**

**Freemasonry:**

# Chapter 48
# Lambskin Apron

As a Masonic tradition, the lambskin apron holds excellent precedence. It is the first Masonic gift given by the Worshipful Master to a candidate. When a Mason symbolically lays down his working tools, it is reverently placed inside his coffin during the funeral and buried with his body. Above all other symbols in Freemasonry, the lambskin apron is considered an honorable Mason badge.

The Entered Apprentice degree elevates its ceremonial white apron in its teaching and points to the garment's inherent virtue and illustrious origins, even more reason a candidate should treat it with dignity and reverence.

At one point during the Entered Apprentice, Fellow-Craft, and Master Mason's degree, the Senior Deacon instructs the candidate how to wear his lambskin apron properly. In Freemasonry, the apron is sometimes made of lambskin because the lamb has always been deemed an emblem of innocence.

# Weekly Guide

**Define Word:**

**Life Situation:**

**Strength:**

**Weakness:**

**Freemasonry:**

# Chapter 49
# Signs and Symbols

Freemasonry uses a variety of Signs and Symbols to communicate its teachings. Additionally, Freemasonry is known for its use of allegories, so signs and symbols often have multiple layers of meaning. Some of the most used signs and symbols include the Square and Compasses, prevalent symbols in Freemasonry. They are often seen in Masonic books, clothing, and temples. The Square represents morality, while the Compasses symbolizes spiritual direction. It is associated with Divine Providence and the belief that God is watching over humanity.

The Letter "G" is often seen in the center of the Square and Compasses and represents God or Geometry. The two columns, Boaz, and Jachin are called "Pillars of Solomon" and are symbols of strength and stability. The Blazing Star symbolizes divine guidance and is often depicted as a five-pointed star. The apron is essential to Freemason's attire and the moral and ethical values central to the organization. It is necessary to note that the meanings and interpretations of these signs and symbols can vary between different Masonic traditions.

Although Freemasonry has been depicted as a universal brotherhood, Harold Dobson, a newly raised Mason, asked the questions at a Masonic in-gathering where many Masons from different states were in attendance, "I've seen rituals conferred from several states, with signs and symbols consistently portrayed; however, rituals were slightly different, but at the completion, all convey the same allegory." He asked why are the rituals different in other states.

# Weekly Guide

**Define Word:**

**Life Situation:**

**Strength:**

**Weakness:**

**Freemasonry:**

# Chapter 50
# Broken Column

The Broken Column is a symbol representing the loss of a Mason. It symbolizes the loss of a pillar of strength and support in the community and serves as a reminder of mortality and the transience of life. The Broken Column typically consists of a broken or shattered column near its top, with the broken pieces at its base. The symbolism of the Broken Column serves as a reminder that despite our best efforts and achievements, we are all subject to the laws of nature and the inevitability of death.

Abraham Levy, a renowned Masonic lecturer, gave a lecture on The Broken Column in which he explained, "The Broken Column represents death and is often depicted as a column that is broken or incomplete, symbolizing the loss of a great builder and the interruption of the building of the temple." The Broken Column is also seen as a symbol of the fragility of life and the importance of cherishing each day, as well as a reminder of the need to continue the work left unfinished.

# Weekly Guide

**Define Word:**

**Life Situation:**

**Strength:**

**Weakness:**

**Freemasonry:**

# Chapter 51
# Past Master

A Past Master of a lodge typically refers to someone previously serving as the Worshipful Master of a Masonic lodge. In Freemasonry, the Worshipful Master is the lodge's highest-ranking officer and leader. Once a Mason has completed their term as Worshipful Master, they are then referred to as a Past Master of the lodge. This title is an honorary one and signifies a level of experience and leadership within the Masonic community. Past Masters often remain active in their lodge and may take on other roles or responsibilities within the Masonic organization.

It is worth noting that Freemasonry has various rites, traditions, and practices that can vary by jurisdiction, so the specifics might differ depending on the Masonic organization and region.

The Past Masters Association of Anywhere Lodge was uncertain about the future direction of their lodge. Some thought the new officers needed to focus more on running the lodge as a business. Other Past Masters thought they should let the new officers lead the lodge toward more technological information geared towards younger members, education and research, retention, and esoteric masonry, and less on bills and fundraisers.

## Weekly Guide

**Define Word:**

**Life Situation:**

**Strength:**

**Weakness:**

**Freemasonry:**

# Chapter 52
# Most Worshipful Grand Master

The Most Worshipful Grand Master is an honorific used in various Masonic organizations worldwide. It typically refers to the highest-ranking officer within a Grand Lodge, the governing body of Freemasonry in a particular jurisdiction (usually a state or a country).

The Most Worshipful Grand Master holds a position of leadership and authority within the Grand Lodge and presides over its meetings and activities. They are responsible for the overall administration and direction of Masonic affairs within their jurisdiction. The exact duties and powers of a Most Worshipful Grand Master can vary depending on the specific rules and regulations of the Grand Lodge they preside over.

It is worth noting that the term Most Worshipful is a form of courtesy and respect within the Masonic fraternity, and it is used regardless of the religious or spiritual beliefs of the individual holding the position.

The Anywhere Grand Lodge of Somewhere Masons was about to ballot on changing the term of the Most Worshipful Grand Master from one year to two years. Before the vote, it had to be put on the floor for a motion, properly second, and then for all the voting members to have an open discussion for those who opposed and those who approved. It was said before the votes were to be cast, brothers govern yourself accordingly.

# Weekly Guide

**Define Word:**

**Life Situation:**

**Strength:**

**Weakness:**

**Freemasonry:**

# References

Brown, D. (2009). *The Lost Symbol: a novel.* New York, Doubleday, p.106.

Coil, H. W. (1961). *Coils Masonic Encyclopedia.* New York, New York, Macoy Publishing and Masonic Supply Company p.270.

Masonic Lodge of Education Masonic Ritual Words in the United States. https://www.Masonic-lodge-of-

McIntosh, M.A. High Moral Standards of Freemasons. West https://www.thesquaremagazine.com/mag/article/202103the-chamber-of-reflection/

Oxford University Press. (2010). *New Oxford American Dictionary 3rd Edition.* Oxford University Press 3rd edition.

Kumar, D. J. (2008). *Freemasons-Freemasonry.com/morality_Freemasonry.html.* Retrieved 4 /4/2022, 2022, from Pietre-Stones Review of Freemasonry.

McEvoy, N. (2011, May 7). The Old Master Wages. *The Educator*, p. 1.

Newton, J. (1973). *The Builders.* Lexington: Supreme Council 33 AASR Northern Masonic District.